POCKET POSITIVES
for
INSPIRATION

POCKET POSITIVES
for
INSPIRATION

An Anthology of Quotations

Summit Press
950 Stud Road, Rowville
Victoria 3178
Australia

Email: publishing@fivemile.com.au
Website: www.fivemile.com.au

First published 2001 as *The Ultimate Pocket Positives*
This revised edition first published 2006

This compilation © The Five Mile Press Pty Ltd

Compiled by Maggie Pinkney
Designed by Zoë Murphy
Illustration by Zoë Murphy
Printed in China

ISBN 1 74178 001 2

CONTENTS

You Can Do It!

Let Nature Enlarge Your Spirit

Light Your Life with Learning

Believe in Miracles

Let Go of Regrets

Call It Luck …

Stop and Ponder Life's Meaning

Love is All You Need

Comforting Words

PREFACE

L et these 'pocket positives' – life-affirming quotations from the world's greatest writers, entertainers, politicians and thinkers – inspire you to greater things.

The distilled wisdom contained in this optimistic anthology can help you maintain a positive attitude, even when things go wrong. We all suffer setbacks from time to time; it's the way we react to them that counts.

Leo Tolstoy once wrote, 'Use the good thoughts of wise people', and this is exactly what this collection of quotations is all about: good thoughts from the wise. Use this concentrated wisdom to help you realize your own potential, and to appreciate all that life has to offer.

Maggie Pinkney, 2006

THE POWER OF ONE

I am only one.

But still I am one.

I cannot do everything,

but still I can do something.

I will not refuse to do

the something I can do.

————————

HELEN KELLER, 1880–1968
American writer and lecturer

My will shall shape my future.

Whether I fail or succeed shall be

no man's doing but my own. I am the force.

I can clear any obstacle before me or

I can be lost in the maze.

My choice, my responsibility. Win or lose,

only I hold the key to my destiny.

ELAINE MAXWELL
American writer

I believe that we are
solely responsible for our choices,
and we have to accept
the consequence of every deed,
word and thought
throughout our lifetime.

—————————

ELISABETH KÜBLER-ROSS, 1926–2004
Swiss-born American psychiatrist

I don't think of myself as a poor,

deprived ghetto girl who made good.

I think of myself as somebody

who from an early age

knew I was responsible for myself,

and I had to make good.

OPRAH WINFREY, b. 1954
American television personality

A single hand's turn given heartily

to the world's great work

helps one amazingly

with one's own small tasks.

LOUISA MAY ALCOTT, 1832–1880
American novelist

There is not enough darkness in the world to extinguish the light of one small candle.

SPANISH PROVERB

However much I am at the mercy of the world,

I never let myself get lost by brooding

over its misery.

I hold firmly to the thought that each one of us

can do a little to bring

some portion of that misery to an end.

ALBERT SCHWEITZER, 1875–1965
French philosopher and physician

There's much to be said
for challenging fate
instead of ducking behind it.

DIANA TRILLING, 1905–1996
American author

You can do or be

whatever you want in your own life.

Nothing can stop you,

except your own fears.

Don't blame anyone else … you have

the power to make the decision.

Just do it.

———————

NOLA DIAMANTOPOULOS
Greek-Australian creative workshop tutor

WHY NOT BE
AN OPTIMIST?

I am an optimist.

It does not seem too much use

being anything else.

—————————

WINSTON CHURCHILL, 1874–1965
British statesman, Prime Minister and writer

All things are possible

until they are proved impossible —

even the impossible

may only be so as of now.

PEARL S. BUCK, 1892–1973
American writer and humanitarian

I have become

my own version of an optimist.

If I can't make it through one door,

I'll go through another door —

or I'll make a door.

Something terrific will come

no matter how dark the present.

JOAN RIVERS, b. 1935
American comedian

Optimism is the faith
that leads to achievement.
Nothing can be done
without hope and confidence.

HELEN KELLER, 1880–1968
American writer and lecturer

The very least you can do in your life

is to figure out what you hope for.

And the most you can do

is to live inside that hope.

Not admire it from a distance

but live right in it, under its roof.

BARBARA KINGSOLVER, b. 1955
American novelist

I am an optimist,

unrepentant and militant.

After all, in order not to be a fool an optimist

must know how sad a place the world can be.

It is only the pessimist

who finds this out anew every day.

———————

PETER USTINOV, 1921–2004
English writer, actor and dramatist

Expect to have hope rekindled.

Expect your prayers

to be answered in wondrous ways.

The dry seasons in life do not last.

The spring rains will come again.

SARAH BAN BREATHNACH
American writer

Optimists are the elixir of life.

They constantly remind the pessimists

that life isn't as hopeless as they think.

They are the extra ingredient

that makes life bubble.

SARA HENDERSON, 1936–2005
Australian outback station manager and writer

For what human ill

does not dawn seem to be

an alleviation?

THORNTON WILDER, 1897–1975
American dramatist and writer

Tomorrow is the most important thing in life.

Comes to us at midnight very clean.

It's perfect when it arrives and it puts itself

in our hands.

It hopes we've learnt something

from yesterday.

JOHN WAYNE, 1907–1979
American screen actor

The only limit

to our realization of tomorrow

will be our doubts of today.

Let us move forward

with strong and active faith.

FRANKLIN D. ROOSEVELT, 1882–1945
President of the United States of America

The optimist is wrong as often
as the pessimist.
But he has a lot more fun.

ANONYMOUS

One of the things I learned the hard way

was that it doesn't pay to get discouraged.

Keeping busy and making optimism a way of life

can restore your faith in yourself.

LUCILLE BALL, 1911–1989
American actress

DOWN BUT NOT OUT

Our greatest glory

is not in never falling,

but in rising

every time we fall.

———————

CONFUCIUS, c. 550–478 BC
Chinese philosopher

My downfall raises me to great heights.

NAPOLEON BONAPARTE, 1769–1821
French emperor and general

When we begin

to take our failures non-seriously,

it means we are ceasing

to be afraid of them.

It is of immense importance

to learn to laugh at ourselves.

KATHERINE MANSFIELD, 1888–1923
New Zealand writer

But what if I fail of my purpose here?

It is but to keep the nerves at a strain,

To dry one's eyes and laugh at a fall,

And, baffled, get up and begin again.

———————

ROBERT BROWNING, 1812–1889
English poet

He's no failure. He's not dead yet.

GWILYM LLOYD GEORGE, 1894–1967
Welsh politician

Austere perseverance,

harsh and continuous, may be

employed by the smallest of us

and rarely fails its purpose,

for its silent power grows

irresistibly greater with time.

———————

JOHANN VON GOETHE, 1749–1832
German poet and writer

Great works are performed

not by strength

but by perseverance.

SAMUEL JOHNSON, 1709–1784
English lexicographer, critic and writer

START BY IMAGINING

All the things we achieve
are things we have
first of all imagined.

DAVID MALOUF, b. 1934
Australian writer

Imagination is the beginning of creation.

You imagine what you desire,

you will what you imagine,

and at last you create

what you will.

GEORGE BERNARD SHAW, 1856–1950
Irish dramatist, writer and critic

Imagination is the highest kite one can fly.

LAUREN BACALL, b. 1924
American actress

Throw your dreams into space like a kite,

and you do not know what it will bring back:

a new life, a new friend, a new love,

a new country.

ANAÏS NIN, 1903–1977
French novelist

Imagination
is more important
than knowledge.

ALBERT EINSTEIN, 1879–1955
German-born American physicist

W ithout leaps of imagination,

or dreaming,

we lose the excitement of possibilities.

Dreaming, after all,

is a form of planning.

GLORIA STEINEM, b. 1934
American feminist and writer

To accomplish great things

we must not only act,

but also dream;

not only plan,

but also believe.

———————

ANATOLE FRANCE, 1844–1924
French writer

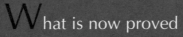

What is now proved

was once only

imagined.

WILLIAM BLAKE, 1757–1827
English poet, artist and mystic

The world is but canvas
to our imagination.

HENRY DAVID THOREAU, 1817–1862
American essayist and social critic

Imagination finds a road
to the realm of the gods,
and there man can glimpse
that which is to be
after the soul's liberation
from the world of substance.

KAHLIL GIBRAN, 1883–1931
Lebanese poet, artist and mystic

Knowledge is limited.

Imagination encircles

the whole world.

ALBERT EINSTEIN, 1879–1955
German-born American physicist

SIMPLE PLEASURES

May I a small house and large garden have.

And a few Friends, and many Books, both true,

Both wise, and both delightful too.

He is happiest,

be he king or peasant,

who finds peace in his home.

———————

JOHANN VON GOETHE, 1749–1832
German poet and writer

The day, water, sun, moon, night —
I do not have to pay
to enjoy these things.

TITUS MACCIUS PLATUS, c. 254–184 BC
Roman dramatist

I like to walk about among

the beautiful things that adorn the world;

but private wealth I should decline,

or any sort of personal possessions,

because they would take away my liberty.

GEORGE SANTAYANA, 1863–1952
Spanish-born American philosopher

If I had two loaves of bread,

I would sell one and buy hyacinths.

For they would feed my soul.

THE QUR'AN

What a delight it is

When, of a morning, I get up and go out

To find in full bloom a flower

That yesterday was not there.

TACHIBANA AKEMI, 1812–1868
Japanese poet

Yes, in the poor man's garden grow

Far more than herbs and flowers —

Kind thoughts, contentment, peace of mind,

And joy for weary hours.

MARY HOWITT, 1799–1888
English poet

Quiet by day,

Sound sleep by night: study and ease

Together mixed; sweet recreation,

And innocence, which most doth please

With meditation.

———————

ALEXANDER POPE, 1688–1744
English poet

O gift of God! a perfect day,

Whereon shall no man work but play,

Whereon it is enough for me

Not to be doing but to be.

———————

HENRY WADSWORTH LONGFELLOW, 1807–1882
American poet and writer

One is nearer
God's Heart in a garden
Than anywhere else on earth.

DOROTHY FRANCES GURNEY, 1858–1932
English poet

Who loves a garden still his Eden keeps,

Perennial pleasures, plants and

wholesome harvest reaps.

———————

AMOS BRONSON ALCOTT, 1799–1888
American teacher and philosopher

GIVE IT YOUR BEST

Believe in the best,

think your best, study your best,

have a goal for your best,

never be satisfied with less than your best,

try your best, and in the long run

things will turn out for the best.

———————

HENRY FORD, 1863–1947
American motor-car manufacturer

Good, better, best,

May you never rest,

Until your good is better,

And your better best.

ANONYMOUS

There is a better way to do it;
find it.

THOMAS A. EDISON, 1847–1931
American inventor

Don't let the best you have done so far
be the standard for the rest of your life.

———————

GUSTAVUS F. SWIFT, 1839–1903
American business magnate

When we do the best we can,

we never know what miracle

is wrought in our life or

the life of another.

HELEN KELLER, 1880–1968
American writer and lecturer

I am easily satisfied
with the very best.

WINSTON CHURCHILL, 1874–1965
British statesman, Prime Minister and writer

I do the very best I know how —

the very best I can;

and I mean to keep on doing it

until the end.

———————

ABRAHAM LINCOLN, 1809–1865
President of the United States of America

GROWTH – AND CHANGE

Growth, in some curious way,

I suspect, depends on being

always in motion just a little bit,

one way or another.

—————

NORMAN MAILER, b. 1923
American writer

We must always change,

renew, rejuvenate ourselves;

otherwise we harden.

JOHANN VON GOETHE, 1749–1832
German poet and writer

Only in growth, reform, and change,

paradoxically enough,

is true security to be found.

ANNE MORROW LINDBERGH, 1906–2001
American writer

Life is change.
Growth is optional.
Choose wisely.

KAREN KAISER CLARK, b. 1938
American legislator and feminist

The old woman I shall become

will be quite different

from the woman I am now.

Another I is beginning.

———————

GEORGE SAND (AMANDINE DUPIN), 1804–1876
French novelist

Every small positive change

we make in ourselves

repays us in confidence

in the future.

ALICE WALKER, b. 1944
American author

We shrink from change; yet is there anything that can come into being without it? What does Nature hold dearer, or more proper to herself? Could you have a hot bath unless the firewood underwent some change? ... Do you not see, then, that change in yourself is of the same order, and no less necessary to Nature.

MARCUS AURELIUS, 121–180 AD
Roman emperor and philosopher

To learn, to desire, to know,

to feel, to think, to act.

This is what I want.

And nothing else.

That is what I must try for.

KATHERINE MANSFIELD, 1888–1923
New Zealand writer

Who is not satisfied with himself

will grow.

HEBREW PROVERB

KEEP YOUR CURIOSITY
ALIVE

A generous and elevated mind

is distinguished by nothing more certainly

than an eminent degree of curiosity.

———————

SAMUEL JOHNSON, 1709–1784
English lexicographer, critic and writer

Curiosity

has its own reason for existing.

Never lose a holy curiosity.

***

ALBERT EINSTEIN, 1879–1955
German-born American physicist

Curiosity is a gift,

a capacity for pleasure in knowing,

which if you destroy,

you make yourselves cold and dull.

———————

JOHN RUSKIN, 1819–1900
English author and art critic

Those with a lively
sense of curiosity
learn something new
every day of their lives.

ANONYMOUS

If I had influence with the good fairy

who is supposed to preside over

the christening of all children, I should ask

that her gift to each child in the world

would be a sense of wonder so indestructible

that it would last throughout life.

RACHEL CARSON, 1907–1964
American biologist and writer

Whoever retains

the natural curiosity of childhood

is never bored or dull.

ANONYMOUS

The important thing is
not to stop questioning.

ALBERT EINSTEIN, 1879–1955
German-born American physicist

For a man who cannot wonder

is but a pair of spectacles

behind which there are no eyes.

THOMAS CARLYLE, 1795–1881
Scottish historian, essayist and critic

Disinterested intellectual curiosity

is the lifeblood of real civilization.

GEORGE MACAULAY TREVELYAN, 1876–1962
British historian

REFLECTIONS ON
GREATNESS

I studied the lives

of great men and famous women,

and I found the men and women

who got to the top were those

who did the jobs they had in hand,

with everything they had of energy

and enthusiasm and hard work.

HARRY S. TRUMAN, 1884–1972
President of the United States of America

No great man lives in vain.

The history of the world is but

the biography of great men.

THOMAS CARLYLE, 1795–1881
Scottish historian, essayist and critic

Great lives never go out.
They go on.

BENJAMIN HARRISON, 1833–1901
President of the United States of America

The heights by great men reached and kept

Were not attained by sudden flight,

But they, while their companions slept,

Were toiling upward in the night.

———————

HENRY WADSWORTH LONGFELLOW, 1807–1882
American poet and writer

One can build the Empire State Building,

discipline the Prussian army,

make a state hierarchy mightier than God,

yet fail to overcome

the unaccountable superiority

of certain human beings.

—————

ALEXANDER SOLZHENITSYN, b. 1918
Russian writer

We are all worms,
but I do believe
I'm a glow-worm.

WINSTON CHURCHILL, 1874–1965
British statesman, Prime Minister and writer

Keep away from people

who try to belittle your ambitions.

Small people always do that,

but the really great make you feel

that you, too, can become great.

MARK TWAIN, 1835–1910
American humorist and writer

There is a great man,

who makes every man feel small.

But the real great man is the man

who makes every man feel great.

G.K. CHESTERTON, 1874–1936
English novelist and critic

The measure of a truly great man

is the courtesy with which

he treats lesser men.

ANONYMOUS

Lives of great men all remind us

We can make our lives sublime,

And, departing, leave behind us

Footprints in the sands of time.

_____

HENRY WADSWORTH LONGFELLOW, 1807–1882
American poet and writer

Great men are the guide-posts and landmarks in the state.

EDMUND BURKE, 1729–1797
British statesman and philosopher

For the courage of greatness

is adventurous and knows not withdrawing,

But grasps the nettle danger, with resolute hands,

And ever again gathers security

from the sting of pain.

VERA BRITTAIN, 1893–1970
English author and poet

Greatness lies not only in being strong,

but in the right use of strength.

HENRY WARD BEECHER, 1813–1887
American clergyman

YOU CAN DO IT!

Achievement is largely

the product of steadily raising

one's level of

aspiration and expectation.

———————

JACK NICKLAUS, b. 1940
American golfer

If you can walk
You can dance.
If you can talk
You can sing.

ZIMBABWEAN PROVERB

To achieve great things

we must live as though we

were never going to die.

LUC DE CLAPIERS, MARQUIS DE VAUVENARGUES, 1715–1747
French moralist and writer

It was a golden year

beyond my dreams.

I proved you're never

too old to achieve

what you really want to do.

───────────

HEATHER TURLAND, b. 1960
Australian Women's Marathon gold medallist

What three things do you
want to accomplish this year?
Write them down and place them
on your refrigerator
for inspiration all year long.

ANONYMOUS

You can have anything you want

if you want it desperately enough.

You must want it with an inner exuberance

that erupts through the skin and

joins the energy that created the world.

SHEILAH GRAHAM, 1904–1988
English-born American gossip columnist

All the strength you need

to achieve anything

is within you.

SARA HENDERSON, 1936–2005
Australian outback station manager and writer

LET NATURE ENLARGE
YOUR SPIRIT

All through my life,

the new sights of Nature

made me rejoice like a child.

———————

MARIE CURIE, 1867–1934
Polish-born French chemist

There can be no very black misery
to him who lives in the midst of nature
and has his senses still.

HENRY DAVID THOREAU, 1817–1862
American writer

Come forth
into the light of things,
Let Nature
be your teacher.

———————

WILLIAM WORDSWORTH, 1770–1850
British poet

After you have exhausted

what there is in business, politics,

conviviality and so on —

what remains?

Nature remains.

WALT WHITMAN, 1819–1892
American poet

There is a pleasure in the pathless woods,

There is a rapture on the lonely shore,

There is society, where none intrudes,

By the deep Sea, and music in its roar.

I love not Man the less, but Nature more.

LORD BYRON, 1788–1824
English poet

Nature never did betray the heart that loved her.

WILLIAM WORDSWORTH, 1770–1850
British poet

Love all God's creation,

both the whole and every grain of sand.

Love every leaf, every ray of light.

Love the animals, love the plants,

love each separate thing.

If thou love each thing thou wilt perceive

the mystery of God in all...

FEODOR DOSTOEVSKY, 1821–1881
Russian novelist

Every part of this earth is sacred to my people.

Every shining pine needle, every sandy shore,

Every mist in the dark woods, every clearing

and every humming insect

is holy in the memory of my people.

CHIEF SEATHL
From a letter written in 1883 to the President of the United States of America

Those undescribed, ambrosial mornings

when a thousand birds were heard

gently twittering and ushering in the light,

like the argument to a new canto

of an epic and heroic poem.

The serenity, the infinite promise

of such a morning...

———————

HENRY DAVID THOREAU, 1817–1862
American writer

LIGHT YOUR LIFE
WITH LEARNING

Learning should be a joy

and full of excitement.

It is life's greatest adventure;

it is an illustrated excursion into the minds

of noble and learned men,

not a conducted tour through a jail.

TAYLOR CALDWELL, 1900–1985
American writer

T he primary purpose

of a liberal education

is to make one's mind

a pleasant place in which

to spend one's leisure.

———————

SYDNEY J. HARRIS, b. 1911
American journalist

Learning makes a man fit company for himself.

THOMAS FULLER, 1608–1661
English cleric and historian

Knowledge and understanding

are life's faithful companions

who will never be untrue to you.

For knowledge is your crown,

and understanding your staff;

and when they are with you,

you can possess no greater treasures.

KAHLIL GIBRAN, 1883–1931
Lebanese poet, artist and mystic

If a man empties

his purse into his head,

no one can take it from him.

BENJAMIN FRANKLIN, 1706–1790
American statesman and scientist

For as the old saying is,

When house and land

are gone and spent

Then Learning is most excellent.

SAMUEL FOOTE, 1720–1777
English actor, dramatist and wit

The roots of education are bitter,
but the fruit is sweet.

ARISTOTLE, 384–322 BC
Greek philosopher

The supreme end of education

is expert discernment in all things –

the power to tell the good from the bad,

the genuine from the counterfeit,

and to prefer the good and genuine

to the bad and counterfeit.

SAMUEL JOHNSON, 1709–1784
English lexicographer, critic and wrietr

Knowledge is power itself.

FRANCIS BACON, 1561–1626
English philosopher and essayist

BELIEVE IN MIRACLES

Miracles seem to me to rest

not so much upon faces or voices or

healing power suddenly near to us from afar off,

but upon our perceptions being made finer,

so that for a moment our eyes can see

and our ears can hear

what is there about us always.

WILLA CATHER, 1876–1947
American writer

I am where I am
because I believe
in all possibilities.

WHOOPI GOLDBERG, b. 1955
American actress

Why, who makes much of a miracle?

As to me I know nothing but miracles –

To me every hour of night and day is a miracle,

Every cubic inch of space a miracle.

WALT WHITMAN, 1819–1892
American poet

Miracles are instantaneous;

they cannot be summoned

but they come of themselves,

usually at unlikely moments

and to those who least expect them.

KATHERINE A. PORTER, 1890–1980
American author

Where there is a great love, there are always miracles.

WILLA CATHER, 1876–1947
American writer

Increasing success,

lasting love and vibrant health

are practical miracles

within everyone's reach.

_____

DR JOHN GREY
American psychiatrist and author

Miracles happen

to those who believe in them.

BERNARD BERENSON, 1865–1959
American art critic

LET GO OF REGRETS

Be not like him

who sits by his fireside

and watches the fire go out,

then blows vainly upon the dead ashes.

Do not give up hope or yield to despair

because of that which is past,

for to bewail the irretrievable

is the worst of human frailties.

KAHLIL GIBRAN, 1883–1931
Lebanese poet, artist and mystic

Regret

is an appalling waste of energy.

You can't build on it;

it is good only for wallowing in.

———————

KATHERINE MANSFIELD, 1888–1923
New Zealand writer

To regret one's own experiences

is to arrest one's own development.

To deny one's own experiences

is to put a lie into the lips of one's own life.

It is no less a denial of the soul.

———————

OSCAR WILDE, 1854–1900
Irish poet, wit and dramatist

To look up and not down,

To look forward and not back,

To look out and not in –

To lend a hand!

―――――――――

EDWARD EVERETT HALE, 1882–1909
American Unitarian clergyman and inspirational writer

Nobody gets to live life backward.

Look ahead,

that is where your future lies.

ANN LANDERS, 1918–2002
American advice columnist

The past cannot be changed.
The future is yet in your power.

MARY PICKFORD, 1893–1979
American silent screen actress

Make it a rule of life never to regret

and never look back.

We all live in suspense,

from day to day, from hour to hour;

in other words, we are the hero

of our own story.

MARY McCARTHY, 1912–1989
American author and critic

God grant me

the serenity to accept the things

I cannot change,

the courage to change

the things I can,

and the wisdom to distinguish

the one from the other.

REINHOLD NIEBUHR, 1892–1971
American theolegian

There's no point dwelling

on what might or could have been.

You just have to go forward.

JACK NICHOLSON, b. 1937
American actor

CALL IT LUCK ...

I am a great believer in luck,

and I find the harder I work

the more I have of it.

———————

STEPHEN LEACOCK, 1869–1944
English-born Canadian economist and humorist

I never knew an early-rising,

hard-working, prudent man,

careful of his earnings,

and strictly honest,

who complained of bad luck.

JOSEPH ADDISON, 1672–1719
English essayist and politician

Shallow men
believe in luck.
Strong men
believe in cause and effect.

———————

RALPH WALDO EMERSON, 1803–1882
American essayist and philosopher

How can you say luck and chance

are the same thing?

Chance is the first step you take,

luck is what comes afterwards.

———————

AMY TAN, b. 1952
Chinese-American writer

Luck is infatuated
with the efficient.

PERSIAN PROVERB

Anyone who does not know

how to make the most of his own luck

has no right to complain

if it passes him by.

———————

MIGUEL DE CERVANTES, 1547–1616
Spanish writer

Luck to me is something else.

Hard work – and realizing

what is opportunity and what isn't.

LUCILLE BALL, 1911–1989
American actress

STOP AND PONDER
LIFE'S MEANING

At the end of your life,

you will never regret

not having passed one more test,

not winning one more verdict

or not closing one more deal.

You will regret time

not spent with a husband, a friend,

a child or parent.

BARBARA BUSH, b. 1925
First Lady of the United States of America

The purpose of life is to matter —

to count, to stand for something,

to have it make some difference

that we lived at all.

LEO ROSTEN, 1908–1997
Polish-born American writer and humorist

The greatest use of life
is to spend it for something
that will outlast it.

WILLIAM JAMES, 1842–1910
American pshychologist and philosopher

No man can live happily

who regards himself alone,

who turns everything to his own advantage.

Thou must live for another

if thou wishest to live for thyself.

SENECA, c. 4 BC–65 AD
Roman philosopher, dramatist and statesman

You must understand the whole of life,

not just one little part of it.

That is why you must read,

that is why you must look at the skies,

that is why you must sing and dance,

and write poems, and suffer;

and understand,

for all that is life.

———————————

JIDDU KRISHNAMURTI, 1895–1986
Indian theosophist

He who does not live

in some degree for others,

hardly lives for himself.

MICHEL DE MONTAIGNE, 1533–1592
French essayist

Each player must accept

the cards life deals him.

But once they are in hand,

he alone must decide

how to play the cards

in order to win the game.

VOLTAIRE, 1694–1778
French philosopher and author

There are two things to aim for in life:

first to get what you want;

and, after that, to enjoy it.

Only the wisest of mankind

achieve the second.

———————————

LOGAN PEARSALL SMITH, 1865–1946
American-born British wit, writer and critic

Life is not made up

of great sacrifices and duties

but of little things in which smiles

and kindness given habitually

are what win and preserve

the heart and secure comfort.

———————

SIR HUMPHRY DAVY, 1778–1829
English chemist and inventor

We have to steer our true life's course.

Whatever your calling is in life!

The whole purpose of being here

is to figure out what that is as soon as possible,

so you go about the business of being on track,

of not being owned by what your mother said,

what society said, whatever people think

a woman is supposed to be...

when you can exceed other people's expectations

and be defined by your own!

OPRAH WINFREY, b. 1954
American television personality

I have never given very deep thought to a philosophy of life, though I have a few ideas that I think are useful to me: Do whatever comes your way as well as you can. Think as little as possible about yourself. Think as much as possible about other people. Dwell on things that are interesting. Since you get more joy out of giving joy to others you should put a good deal of thought into the happiness that you are able to give.

ELEANOR ROOSEVELT, 1884–1962
First Lady of the United States of America, writer and diplomat

Is it so small a thing

to have enjoy'd the sun,

to have liv'd light

In the spring, to have lov'd,

to have thought,

to have done?

MATTHEW ARNOLD, 1822–1888
English poet and essayist

As long as you live,

keep learning how to live.

—————

SENECA, c. 4 BC – 65 AD
Roman dramatist, poet and statesman

LOVE IS ALL YOU NEED

To love

means never to be afraid of the windstorms of life;

should you shield the canyons from the windstorms

you would never see the beauty of the carvings.

ELISABETH KÜBLER-ROSS, 1926–2004
Swiss-born American psychiatrist and writer

Treasure the love that you receive

above all.

It will survive long after

your gold and good health

have vanished.

OG MANDINO, 1923–1996
American author

The only thing I know about love
is that love is all there is...
Love can do all
but raise the dead.

EMILY DICKINSON, 1830–1886
American poet

Love is a fruit in season at all times,

and within the reach of every hand.

Anyone may gather it and no limit is set.

Everyone can reach this love through meditation,

spirit of prayer, and sacrifice,

by an intense inner life.

MOTHER TERESA OF CALCUTTA, 1910–1997
Yugoslav-born missionary

In our life

there is a single color,

as on an artist's palette,

which provide the meaning

of life and art.

It is the color of love.

———————

MARC CHAGALL, 1887–1985
French artist

One word frees us

of all the weight and pain of life;

that word is love.

SOPHOCLES, 496–406 BC
Greek tragedian

There is a land of the living

and a land of the dead,

and the bridge is love.

THORNTON WILDER, 1897–1975
American dramatist and writer

Love is patient,

love is kind.

It does not envy,

it does not boast,

it is not proud.

It is not rude,

it is not self-seeking,

it is not easily angered,

it keeps no records of wrongs.

―――――

CORINTHIANS 13: 4-5

If we make our goal to live

a life of compassion and unconditional love,

then the world will indeed become

a garden where all kinds of flowers

can bloom and grow.

ELISABETH KÜBLER-ROSS, 1926–2004
Swiss-born American psychiatrist and writer

COMFORTING WORDS

And this for comfort thou must know:

Times that are ill won't still be so;

Clouds will not ever pour down rain;

A sullen day will clear again.

ROBERT HERRICK, 1591–1674
English poet

It is always darkest
just before
the day dawneth.

THOMAS FULLER, 1608–1661
English cleric and historian

And remember,

we all stumble,

every one of us.

That's why it's a comfort

to go hand in hand.

EMILY KIMBROUGH, 1899–1989
American writer

Whenever I have found that I have blundered or that my work has been imperfect, and when I have been contemptuously criticized and even when I have been overpraised, so that I have felt mortified, it has been my greatest comfort to say hundreds of times to myself that 'I have worked as hard and as well as I could, and no man can do more than this'.

CHARLES DARWIN, 1809–1882
British scientist

In the midst of winter,
I finally learned
that there was in me
an invincible summer.

ALBERT CAMUS, 1913–1960
French writer

Expect trouble as an inevitable part of life,

and when it comes, hold your head high,

look it squarely in the eye and say,

'I will be bigger than you. You cannot defeat me.'

Then repeat to yourself

the most comforting words of all,

'This too will pass.'

ANN LANDERS, 1918–2002
American advice columnist